How to Survive the Death of the Dollar:

Preparing for Armageddon: Financial Collapse, Natural Disasters, Nuclear Strikes, the Zombie Apocalypse, and Every Other Threat to Human Life on Earth

William Brocius

Copyright © 2022
William Brocius
All rights reserved.
ISBN: 978-9-69-339229-6 E-book
ISBN: 978-9-69-339230-2 Paperback
ISBN: 978-9-69-339231-9 Hardcover

Disclaimer:

The information provided in this book is for informational, educational and entertainment purposes only. This book contains humor, parody, and satire. Neither the publisher nor the author shall be held liable or responsible for any loss or damage allegedly arising from any suggestion or information contained in this book. We have included this disclaimer for our protection, on the advice of legal counsel.

The author and distributor individually or corporately, do not accept any responsibility for any liabilities resulting from the actions of any parties involved.

Dedication

To all those who have been told to "wait out the stock market crash" by so-called professionals, only to witness their financial dreams and security crumble before their eyes.

To those who have suffered devastating losses and never fully recovered, left to pick up the pieces and forge a new path forward.

To the courageous truth seekers and speakers, the ones who have been persecuted and silenced for daring to question the mainstream narrative and seek a better way.

This book is for you. May it offer you hope, guidance, and the resilience to survive the death of the dollar, empowering you to reclaim control over your financial destiny.

Together, we will forge a new path, one that leads to financial stability and security in an uncertain world.

Acknowledgments

I would like to express my deepest gratitude to the following enigmatic figures who have contributed to the creation of this book in ways that remain shrouded in mystery:

The Cryptic Cartographer - Your whispered guidance led me through uncharted territory, allowing me to uncover hidden truths.

The Shadow Broker - Your unparalleled access to privileged information opened my eyes to the secrets lurking behind the scenes.

The Silent Watcher - Your quiet vigilance and support provided me with the courage to delve deeper into the unknown.

The Unseen Mentor - Your invisible hand steered me in the right direction when I was lost in the maze of conflicting narratives.

The Enigmatic Economist - Your uncanny ability to decipher complex financial patterns has been an invaluable asset in my quest for understanding.

The Nameless Historian - Your uncredited research and dedication to unearthing the buried past have shed light on the recurring cycles of economic upheaval.

The Arcane Archivist - Your meticulous preservation of ancient wisdom has granted me access to the knowledge of ages long forgotten.

The Reclusive Philosopher - Your thought-provoking discussions have challenged me to question the nature of our economic reality.

The Anonymous Insider - Your covert leaks of sensitive information have allowed me to pierce through the veil of deception that clouds our financial system.

The Secret Society - Your clandestine network of like-minded individuals has offered me refuge and camaraderie in the pursuit of truth.

To all of you, who have chosen to remain in the shadows, I offer my most profound appreciation. Your mysterious contributions have been instrumental in the creation of this book, and your influence will be felt by all who seek solace in its pages.

Contents

Introduction

Most Americans haven't thought long and hard about surviving a major disaster. The reason for this is that major disasters are seen as rare; "tail risks" that happen infrequently. But when they do take place, the impact is unmistakable and potentially terminal.

In addition to living life according to normalized expectations, it's important to be aware of and prepare for tail risks in case they do happen. And if you look back at history, major turning points—many of which can be seen as tragic—happen more frequently than most people think. Take the most recent examples:

- 2000: Dot Com Crash
- 2001: September 11, 2001 Terrorist Attacks
- 2008: Global Financial Crisis
- 2009: European Sovereign Debt Crisis
- 2010: Fukushima Nuclear Disaster
- 2014: Crude Oil Crisis

- 2016: BREXIT
- 2016: US-China Trade War
- 2019: Another Crude Oil Crisis
- 2020: COVID-19 Pandemic
- 2021: Global Inflation
- 2022: January 6 Storming of the US Capitol
- 2022: Russia-Ukraine War
- 2023: The Bifurcation of the Global Economy?
- 2023: Introduction of Central Bank Digital Currencies?

These are just a few of the more well-known "Black Swans" to hit the globe. They don't include many of the domestic crises (such as natural disasters) that happen on an almost annual basis. All the examples above have impacted citizens across the globe along with the global economy.

There's a major disaster just around every corner. To obsess over the next potential disaster may be considered an unhealthy form of paranoia. But to ignore them completely and remain unprepared is to actively pursue fragility. Always be prepared. It's better to mistake a stone for a bear than a bear for a stone.

The American Empire Will Collapse

Unless you live in a place where disastrous events like hurricanes, earthquakes, or military conflicts happen on a regular basis, major disasters are things that happen elsewhere, or to other people. Images of disasters are what we see on the news or in movies, but never at home.

In the US, we live in an empire whose roots in democracy have stood for over two centuries. Yet all empires eventually come to end. And while America has had its ups and downs, its victories and near-misses, we can never get so complacent as to ignore the warning signs that our end may be near.

Losing sleep over such a horrifying prospect isn't the smartest way to deal with this level of reality should it indeed materialize. It's all about being prepared and adapting to any environment that can come your way. And this is what the book you're reading is all about: preparation.

A Survival Guide in Two Parts

Part I - The Death of the Dollar

This section concerns financial disasters; the roots of which are taking hold of our financial system now. The "apocalypse" doesn't always materialize from nothing or arrive from nowhere. Often, you can see its signs if you know where to look. Most people don't, so we'll point them out to you in the first section.

It's important to note that in this section, the world is still functioning, though its economy is beginning to crumble. Economic turmoil often precedes societal collapse. Yet financial preparation can place you in a stronger position once society collapses. So, in a sense, the first part of the book prepares you for the second part, which focuses on survival after civilization as we know it has ceased to exist.

Part II - Surviving Apocalypse

Once governmental authority and society has come loose at the seams, your scope of survival will have become "localized" and "material."

As a localized event, you will rely solely on your family, close friends, and neighbors, especially if long-range communication technologies are no longer functional.

Your survival will depend on your capacity to maintain a material level of existing: seeking shelter, food, and means to physically protect yourself. Most people have neither the mindset or skills to survive in the wild. If you are to survive this condition of existence, you will have to develop this mindset and these skills fast. The second part of this book will tell you almost everything you need to know to build and strengthen this capacity.

Part I - The Death of the US Dollar

The US dollar's reign as the world's reserve currency is coming to an end. When it does, the value of every single dollar you hold will be significantly weakened. The worst-case scenario is that the dollar may go to zero. This is unlikely, but its imminent weakening will still be severe enough to destroy the wealth of individuals and households across the country, possibly to the point of social unrest and civil war.

How so? The US will no longer enjoy superior purchasing power. Considering how much of its manufacturers import, this will cause prices to skyrocket beyond common affordability. In the end, high prices will trigger a massive wave of hunger and impoverishment, both of which will lead to crime and social unrest.

Still, you can prepare for such a calamity, in whatever form it comes first. There are plenty of signs, and numerous developments to keep an eye on. Fortunately, your individual solution to hedge against all of it is simple. We'll go over this next.

Just remember: There will be a time when basic wealth = survival. And we believe that time is coming soon.

The Tyranny of Central Bank Digital Currencies

The beginning of the end for most empires is very subtle and often undetected. In many cases, it begins with simple maladjustment in the economy. A currency is inflated, a government goes into deficit spending, or financial rules have been imposed that severely limit the freedoms of its citizens.

These conditions are currently emerging now in a form that's least expected: central bank digital currencies, or CBDCs for short. It's also referred to as the "digital dollar" and its emergence will be justified under the banners of social equity, convenience, economic efficiency, and international competition.

The world is going digital. Fiat money is no exception to digitization. CBDCs are a form of digital fiat money. They will be controlled by central banks; in our case, the Federal Reserve. Americans will not need to have an account at a commercial bank for all CBDCs will be stored with the Federal Reserve.

CBDCs provide convenience in that your money will not have to be transferred using third-party institutions. This way, you avoid all of the extraneous fees for which the banking system is notorious. CBDCs are also a necessity in the realm of international trade. If all major economies are using digital currencies for cross-border payments, then any economy without one will be left behind.

But there's a negative side to CBDCs. They're not private and they're controlled by the central bank and the government. This means they can intrusively track and monitor every dollar you have and every dollar you spend. Your transactions will be recorded, organized and surveilled using an AI system.

More frighteningly, the Fed can create as many dollars as it wishes, often at the behest of the government, which will devalue the money you hold. If the Fed wants you to spend money to boost the economy, it can impose **negative interest rates** so that any money sitting in your account will begin to depreciate the longer it remains unused.

The bottom line here is that your financial freedom and privacy will be 100% gone.

So, how can you possibly survive this? The solution is simple: Hold currencies whose values are globally recognized but that remain out of the government's domain. In short, hold physical gold and silver coins or bars and keep them stored in a safe private depository.

Surviving BRICS

If you're not familiar with the acronym BRICS, it stands for Brazil, Russia, India, China, and South Africa. Argentina has also applied for membership and Saudi Arabia has also expressed interest in joining the group.

When Russia invaded Ukraine in 2021, the western world levied an unprecedented level of sanctions against the country in the hopes of crippling its economy. This had a profound effect on many countries, particularly neutral ones, across the globe.

It showed many countries that the dollar's hegemonic position in the world economy left them vulnerable to the West. If they do anything counter to the West's wishes, their economies will be subject to severe punitive actions. Not surprisingly, many countries began de-dollarizing to get free of the dollar's shackles.

In the summer of 2022, China announced that the BRICS alliance has developed its own international reserve currency to compete with and supplant the US dollar. One of our strongest allies, Saudi Arabia, has expressed interest in joining BRICS. Not only does this threaten to split the world economy into two major monetary factions, it also threatens global confidence in the US dollar.

The main threat here is that all of the dollars you hold in your bank may quickly lose monetary value, leaving you with a fraction of the wealth you once held. And what does BRICS have to back its value against the US dollar? It's gold-backed. So, your dollars will lose its "money value" while the BRICS gold-backed currency will not. The solution to this is to hold gold; plain and simple.

Collapse of Digital Financial Infrastructure

Hurricane Ian wrought damage across Puerto Rico and Florida. But its impact on financial infrastructure this time around wasn't as bad as hurricanes Irma and Maria in 2017.

With ATMs rendered inoperable, people were unable to withdraw cash. Plus, their local government policies were designed to limit physical cash usage. So, after the hurricanes hit, Puerto Rican citizens had no means to buy basic necessities such as food and water.

In the event of a similar infrastructure crisis—a hurricane, EMP bomb, nuclear emergency, social upheaval, or what have you—it makes sense to have cash on hand. And if infrastructure collapse coincides with a severe devaluation of the local currency or hyperinflation, then it makes sense to hold physical currencies, like gold and silver, that rise in value when currencies fall.

When Banks Fail

If you thought the Dodd–Frank Wall Street Reform and Consumer Protection Act of 2010 is there to save you from the kind of Too-Big-To-Fail bank collapses we saw in 2008, then think again.

Buried in the Dodd-Frank Act and concealed by "legalese" is Title II notoriously known as the "Orderly Liquidation Authority," or OLA for short. According to a US Treasury Department report released in February of 2018, it reads: "Treasury recommends retaining OLA as an emergency tool for use under only extraordinary circumstances."

The "extraordinary circumstances" it refers to is the event of a banking crisis.

Title II essentially allows the banking system to freeze your funds and take 50% or more of it in order to save the bank's balance sheets, similar to what happened in Cyprus during their financial crisis in 2012. In exchange, you will receive shares of stock, but for a failing bank.

Here's the main point: The money you keep in your bank is NOT YOURS. It belongs to the bank. And should a bank fail, it has the legal authority to CONFISCATE YOUR MONEY and convert it into the bank's operational funds. It's legal theft. And if you think the FDIC is there to protect your funds, it is but under certain conditions. Judging by the required timing and paperwork you will have to deal with to get your money back, the process favors the banks and not its depositors.

This is why "smart money" always diversifies its wealth in physical gold and silver. The banking system and Wall Street is rigged against the average person.

Remember, when banks mismanage their operations and lose billions of dollars of their and their depositors' funds, they get bailed out. But when you mismanage your funds and default on your payments, however small that amount may be, the government will allow you to go bankrupt.

So, how do you avoid losing all of your money in the event of a bank failure? Don't store all of your money in a bank. Keep it in a secure depository and convert a good portion of it into physical gold and silver. In this way, you won't lose your money and your money won't lose its monetary value.

Banks Can Legally Confiscate Your Savings Deposit

You're probably not aware that if your bank collapses, it's legally authorized to seize 50% or more of your funds thanks to| Dodd-Frank Title II - Orderly Liquidation Authority (OLA).

The money you deposit in your bank no longer belongs to you; it belongs to the bank. The day you've become a "depositor," you've unwittingly agreed to become an "unsecured creditor." This means that your bank can use your funds a*s its own* to avoid insolvency in the event of a major emergency.

Of course, you can avoid this from happening. After all, the FDIC's role is to ensure that your deposited funds are protected up to a certain amount. It's not 100% true: even the FDIC is in on rigging the game.

Case in point: take a look at the following agreements…

Bank of America's <u>Deposit Agreement </u>(Page 9):

In the event of Bank failure, you agree to:

- Cooperate fully with us and the FDIC in connection with determining the insured status of funds in such accounts at any time;
- Provide the FDIC with the information described below in the required format promptly; and
- Submit claims for pass-through insurance to the FDIC through an alternative recordkeeping process.

Note that most banks require you to respond within 24 hours, yet Bank of America fails to disclose this potentially critical requirement--substituting the vague term "promptly" instead. Plus, you are expected to have read and understood three bullet points from a document that has a total word count well over 20,000!

Chase Bank's <u>DEPOSIT ACCOUNT AGREEMENT AND PRIVACY NOTICE</u> (Page 23):

"In the event of a bank failure, you agree to provide the FDIC with the information described above in the required format within 24 hours of a bank failure...You understand and agree that your failure to provide the necessary data to the FDIC may result in a delay in receipt of insured funds."

You are expected to have read and understood two sentences (54 words) from a document that has a total word count of 25,121!

Citibank's <u>Marketplace Addendum</u> (Page 1):

"In the event that Citibank fails, you agree to cooperate fully with us and the FDIC in connection with determining the insured status of funds in such accounts. **This includes providing the FDIC with**

19

the information described above in the required format within 24 hours of bank failure. You understand and agree that your failure to provide the necessary data to the FDIC may result in a delay in your receipt of FDIC insured funds."

You are expected to have read and understood three sentences (75 words) from a document that has a total word count of 24,018!

US Bank's <u>Your Deposit Account Agreement</u> (Page 16):

"You agree to cooperate fully with us and the FDIC in connection with determining the insured status of funds in such accounts at any time. In the event of failure of U.S. Bank, **you agree to provide the FDIC with the information described above in the required format within 24 hours of the failure of U.S. Bank.**"

You are expected to have read and understood two sentences (59 words) from a document that has a total word count of 35,385!

THE BOTTOM LINE IS THAT YOU HAVE 24 HOURS TO NOTIFY THE FDIC OR YOUR FUNDS WILL BE CONFISCATED!

Why didn't you know about this? It's likely buried in your depositor agreement. Check it now. It's likely buried deep within a wall of words ten thousand or more deep. The FDIC is not your friend. It's on the side of Wall Street. And it too is helping rig the game in favor of the banks.

How might you avoid confiscation of your funds? First, check your depositor agreement. Second, stash a portion of your cash (that you couldn't afford to lose) in a private depository. Third, consider diversifying your wealth in safe-haven assets like physical gold and silver (coins or bars) and safely store them in a private depository.

The FDIC Has Been Corrupted by Socialist Ideology

In 2021, Jelena McWilliams, an FDIC member and director of the Consumer Financial Protection Bureau who was nominated by former President Trump, resigned her FDIC post following a Democrat-led "hostile takeover" of the institution.

The FDIC's primary purpose is to insure customer deposits. It also has a hand in overseeing all of the nation's banks. So, what does this have to do with policing bank mergers and pushing the industry to prepare for climate change? This is government intrusion, and the FDIC has now become yet another instrument in the government's coercive arsenal.

From another section in this book, we explain how the FDIC's protections against bank failure are written in language that's nearly impossible for depositors to understand let alone find (it's written in legalese and buried within hundreds of pages of consumer disclosures). The FDIC is there to protect the banking system and the government's interests. It's not there to protect your interest as a consumer and depositor. And with socialist ideology now infecting the almost century-old institution, your money is at even greater risk now than it was in previous years. Unless you're willing to risk your hard-earned wealth, especially in the event of a national emergency, it's in your interest to stash your money away from the banking system and convert a good portion of your dollars to physical gold and silver.

Beware the Socialists in the US Federal Reserve

The Federal Reserve is the bank of all commercial banks in America, yet its influence is strong enough to sway economies across the globe. The Fed has a monopoly on all money issuance. Only they have the legal right to print money or take it out of the money supply. They set interest rates, making money cheaper or more expensive to borrow. None of the Fed's governors were ever voted into office by American citizens. They were nominated by US presidents and confirmed by the Senate.

The current VIce Chair of the Federal Reserve is Lael Brainard. In 2019, prior to taking her current seat as Vice Chair, Rep. Roger Williams asked her a simple question: "Are you a capitalist or a socialist." She refused to answer three times. In other words, she's enough of a socialist to avoid answering the question, as it would have fared poorly with the Senate.

In recent years, the Fed has taken on matters of social equity as an addition to its current dual mandate of supporting maximum employment and price stability. Social equity is a liberal-verging-on-socialist mandate that has infected our nation's top bank.

We covered central bank digital currencies (CBDCs) in another section. In a nutshell, should the Fed launch a CBDC program, that would spell the end of physical cash. All forms of money in the US would be digitized. This means the Fed and government can force you to spend when it wants (by implementing negative interest rates on the money you "save" in your account), and it can inflate the money supply immediately as it wishes. So, if Congress ends up having a socialist majority, it can print as much money as it wishes to pay for its programs. Meanwhile, the value of your dollars will sink to the point where you won't be able to afford much of anything. Remember that money printing is a hidden form of taxation.

How do you avoid this form of financial submission? Secretly stash physical gold and silver coins and keep it away from the government's reach. This way, you can engage in transactions with others who wish to barter or purchase your coins. Meanwhile, the value of your coins will rise far above the value of digital dollars.

Financial Strategies

If you think it is tough to make ends meet in today's economy, wait until the bottom has fallen out of everything! If you don't have some financial strategies in place to work with, you may end up without what you need.

Since you really don't know how it is all going to play out, have several of these financial strategies in place so that you can use one if the other isn't a good fit for a given scenario. These are some financial strategies that may work for you during the difficult times:

Is it Theft?

It was mentioned in a previous chapter that challenging times call for creative responses. Is it really theft if you break into a store to get food or to get medicine? All of those rules are out the window when it comes to the ultimate quest of survival. You need to take what you need before someone else comes along and gets it.

The speed with which such items will disappear depends on the type of scenario that has occurred. For example, with a natural disaster there could be destruction that ruins much of it or the building collapses and it isn't safe to go into them. If there are many people that survive then those items are going to disappear quickly so you need to get to them as soon as you can.

In the event of anarchy or a government control issue,

many of those points where you can get supplies will be monitored and guarded. They will do all they can to keep people from getting to them as they know you can't survive without such items, unless you have prepared well.

Taking a vehicle you need in order to get from your home to a safe place during a disaster shouldn't be classified as theft. Again, you do what you must in order to get through the ordeal. With that in mind, you can use anything you can think of as a means of financial opportunity. As long as you and the other party agree to it, then there is nothing standing in the way.

Cash

You need to have a good amount of cash stored away that can be used in the event of a catastrophe. Remember, the technology we know may be gone so that means going to the bank to make a withdrawal, driving up to the ATM, or relying on credit/debit cards is out the window.

It is best to have many denominations and not to keep all of your cash in one place. If you need to buy a tire for example from a shop, they may tell you it is $60 but if all you have is $100 then they may tell you they don't have change and you have lost out on that cash. Be ready for anything when the world has changed so drastically.

If it takes a very long time for society to be restored after the event has occurred, then cash isn't going to really make too much of a difference overall. People will be more interested in supplies and shelter than money because they aren't going to be able to do much with that cash as the trickle down occurs. Initially though, money can help you get through the first few days or weeks of an emergency situation.

Gold & Silver Coins and Bars

If you have valuables such as bars of gold, silver coins, or precious gems, you may be able to trade them to get what you really need. Someone may be interested in them in exchange for extra firewood they have. In reality, you are getting something far more valuable because it will help you to survive.

Having such items that you can use as payment really does help you to get what you need. Even in times when the world may be coming to an end, people do like to have pretty things!
Commodities

If you have extra items of food that you don't need, you can exchange them for items you do need. Perhaps you are out of water purification pills but you still have lots of water. You can exchange some of that water or some of your food supply to someone that does have those water purification pills on hand. It is a winning outcome for both of you

During stressful times, alcohol may become a prime item that people are looking for. They may be willing to trade you food or even clothing in order to get a few bottles of very good vodka that you have with you. Medical supplies can be in high demand too. If you have extra items that you can spare they may be willing to provide you with other resources you are short on or completely lacking.

Be careful when it comes to offering weapons though that someone may need. You may find yourself in a position later on where you wish you had that gun or that knife with you. The same is very true about offering ammo or arrows in exchange for items because such weaponry supplies are going to be so hard to get your hands on.

Bartering

Along the same lines is the idea of bartering. This is how many people did business back in the days before there was paper money. It involves agreeing to exchange one item that you have for something that another person has. Make sure you get the best possible deal before you come to a final agreement.

It never hurts to try to get them to toss in something extra or to reduce what you give them in exchange for what you want or need. Start out with both of you stating what you have and what you want or need then you can make negotiations from there.

If you aren't around many people though bartering

may be more difficult. With these challenges ahead of you, take what you can if businesses or homes aren't attended. Only barter if you really need something that another person has. Try not to give up anything of value that you really need now or in the future either.

Part II - Surviving Apocalypse

Most of us have thought about how we would handle various types of scenarios that could signal the end of the world. There are plenty of movies on the subject, psychological papers, and even survivalists that are part of reality TV shows. Perhaps you have had dreams about being one of the few left and what you would do in order to survive.

It doesn't matter If think that the chances of a zombie apocalypse are next to zero. There are plenty of other types of scenarios that can occur. There may be a meteor in space that creates serious damages her on Earth. Even though nuclear weapons seem to be more controlled than in the 80's, that doesn't mean the risk of nuclear war is off the table.

What about the risks of natural disasters that are devastating in terms of the volume of damage that they can create? In recent years, the number of tornadoes, hurricanes, and other natural disasters have continued to increase. There can be many reasons for this including changes in overall climate.

You can make yourself crazy though and lose sleep thinking about the what ifs. A better way to handle all of it is to prepare for the worst case scenario. Hopefully, you would never need to have such items put to use. Yet if you do, you will significantly increase your chances of survival.

We live in a society where it seems so easy to get what you need that we take for granted how tough it would play out with a huge disaster. No more buying what you need online or walking into a grocery store for food. No more electricity when you flip a switch or running water when you turn on the faucet.

While we can't control the events that may one day unfold, we can control how we are prepared for them. With some basic items stored, you can have an upper hand on many other people that failed to get anything in place. Creating some types of allies that you would be able to depend on if you had a need during such time could make the difference between life and death.

Weapons may play a large role in who is able to survive and who isn't. Not only in terms of hunting for food, but also in self-protection. In the event of some form of aliens, mutations, or zombies, you need to be able to destroy them. The other issue is that other humans may try to come and take your food, shelter, and supplies if you don't have weapons to keep them away.

Your overall health and well-being are important at every stage of life. During an end of the world scene, you won't be able to just walk into the doctor's office or to get medications. Being fit mentally and physically can help you to be prepared for survival mode

You may be able to stay in your home, but what if you have to make shelter on the go? You need to have a plan A, plan B, variations for different scenarios, and the ability to adapt to what is going on around you. Depending on the situation, you may need to survive for only a few days but you may need to fully care for yourself and your family for months or even years before society is able to regroup.

There is plenty to think about in order to be prepared for anything. The end of the world may never happen in your lifetime, but what if it does? Will you be among those that are prepared and can survive? Will you be able to keep your family safe and to help them thrive in spite of all of it?

In future chapters, you will get a clear idea of what you need in order to achieve such a goal. Think of it like pieces of a puzzle. In order for the picture to look like it should, you need to have every single piece in place. Being prepared means you can stop worrying about it and you can focus on what is going on in your life that you can control.

The Emergence of Reptilian Humanoid DNA

The idea of the "lizard brain" has become a common theme in many popular schools of thought, from finance to social engineering. It began as a metaphor for the human brain stem, the most "primitive" part of the brain that's responsible for impulse and instinct versus rational thought.

The problem is that there is an emerging cult in society that is taking this metaphor too far, elevating this figure of speech to the level of program and function. They are strongly advocating "entomophagy," or the dietary consumption of bugs. Even worse, rumors that some of these advocates are devising ways to fuse reptilian and human DNA are spreading; experiments that are being covered up by authorities who are secretly members of this nefarious cult.

The "reptilian humanoid" is still an emerging phenomenon. Regardless, it's a threat to "natural" human existence. If you suspect such activities taking place, don't just mention your suspicions to anyone lest you're 100% certain that they're not part of this underground society. Here's what to do:

- Don't let the cult detect that you're on to their activities.
- Contact only individual authorities you know well (a law enforcement officer, politician, pastor, local newspaper or media, etc.) and express your concerns.
- The most you can accomplish is full exposure of these reptilian cultists to society.
- Let the authorities handle any forthcoming investigations in a legal manner that's compliant with local and federal regulations.

Necrobotics and the Real Zombie Apocalypse

When we think of zombies, movies or TV shows like *The Night of the Living Dead* or *The Walking Dead* come to mind. A zombie is a dead body that's been reanimated, functioning with a denatured impulse, and without the mind of its original inhabitant. In other words, it's a fantasy world that's separated from our own personal experiences by the partitions of reality.

But how far off from reality is it? With the aid of science, robotics, and pharmaceutical technologies, zombification has already begun. It just looks very different from what we'd expect.

On July 22, 2022, scientists at Rice University successfully reanimated a dead spider for use as a gripping mechanism using the simplest robotic principles and tools: a needle, glue, and a syringe.

Describing this process, the Verge writes "Why bother to design your own robots when you can just reuse what nature created?" That's a frightening prospect. Will advancements in robotics put us in a position wherein dead human bodies can be recycled and reused? That's zombification.

The World Economic Forum's founder, Klaus Schwab, is always raising the notion of the "transhuman." It's essentially a new race defined by neuro-technological brain enhancements and genetic editing among other biotech innovations. It expresses a desire for a new world order controlled (of course) by none other than the elites who have access to this technology. In this new world, we get another form of zombification: natural humans who do not have these enhancements.

Whether we're talking human modifications or the biorobotic reanimation, both "technologies' are designed to enhance the power of a centralized authority. So, in a sense, the "zombie apocalypse" has already begun, with two forms of zombification: one that concerns the denaturing of the human mind and body and another that's biorobotic. Both forms can be prevented on the political level.

Anything can Happen

Being unprepared is the biggest downfall of most people when it comes to surviving the end of the world. If you think nothing major is ever going to happen, you may be thinking differently when it is too late! Don't say that someday you will get ready for the unknown, make it a priority to be ready for anything.

There can be a very short window of time between what you are doing right now and when a disaster occurs. You aren't going to have time to be able to reach out for supplies or to make a plan of action. You don't want to end up in a panic because you aren't sure what to do or because you know you lack skills or supplies.

Have the mindset that anything can happen, and know that you will be ready to face it head on. Take actions that allow you to feel safe, secure, and ready for the future no matter what it may bring your direction. Go over meeting locations, supply options, and more with your family and with friends that you consider allies.

You can be stronger as a team than individually. Don't wait until something has occurred to find out who you can count on. Remember, your supplies will run out fast if you are helping those that weren't prepared.

Here is a list of things that you should be ready for:

- Anarchy

- Artificial Intelligence

- Asteroids

- Chemical war

- Earthquake

- Food storage

- Government Martial Law

- Hurricane (depending on where you live)

- Nuclear war

- Social unrest

- Tsunami (depending on where you live)

- Water shortage

Anarchy

Not everyone is happy with the laws as they are. There is plenty of controversy and taking matters into a new direction may occur. This is known as anarchy and with a large enough group with a similar vision, they would possibly be able to take over and run things their way.

Of course without a balance of laws and regulations, there would be all out riots, battles, and more that would result in plenty losing their lives and only a small percentage surviving.

Artificial Intelligence

Technology offers us many benefits, and computers are very advanced compared to just a decade ago. Some experts feel that we need to worry about artificial intelligence taking over the world. Is it possible that they would one day be able to think on their own?

What if they were programmed with some ulterior motives that a human wasn't able to control or stop? In such a scenario, it would be very difficult to survive without lots of skills and supplies.

Asteroids

There are movements out there in space all the time, and we tend to never worry about them. Yet it is possible for an asteroid to create some type of explosion. Another worry that could occur is that with all of the human disruption of space such as with rockets, satellites, etc. that it is possible for us to create a cosmic chain reaction of events that result in havoc on Earth.

Chemical war

The risk of chemical war could be intentional or by accident. Yet the exposure of such chemicals to living things would certainly destroy most of them. There are several movies that explore this option. For some reason, there would be those that were resistant to the problem. The use of gas masks and other devices could mean the difference between living or dying.

Earthquake

Movement of the Earth at the core or the mantle can result in areas of mass touching each other. This is what creates an Earthquake. The severity of it depends on many factors. Some scientists believe that the end of the world will be due to the many underlying changes to the Earth and the core of it and how it is comprised.

As a result, a very large Earthquake may be one of the ways in which the end of the world happens. There could be a big enough shift in the core and the mantle due to global warming and other negative elements to make it possible, even if only a very small percentage of possibility is there.

Food Shortage

An ecological imbalance could result in a food shortage. This can include overpopulation, changes in climate that make growing food difficult, Deforestation, and even lack of fish due to pollution in the waterways. A lack of food would have a chain reaction for both humans and animals.

Government Martial Law

It is no secret that the economy is in dire straits, and it has been that way for quite some time. Government martial law may occur at some point, and only those that are really ready for it would be able to survive. This type of tactic would include a curfew, rations on food, relocation that is by force, and even supplies and weapons being confiscated.

Hurricane (depending on where you live)

Tropical storms and hurricanes can occur in areas where there are large bodies of water close by the coast. They can create huge amounts of high winds combined with the force of high waters onto the land. While it is unlikely that a hurricane could create enough devastation for the end of the world, they could cause enough damage in locations that it could have a serious trickle down effect for those that do survive.

Nuclear War

There are counter measures in place for nuclear weapons, and the ability to steer them off course. However, that is all in theory though and never really tested in an actual event scenario. The ability to track nuclear weapons though via satellite has significantly reduced the chances of such a doomsday event wiping out the majority of humanity. Still, it can't be entirely ruled out of the equation.

Social Unrest

Significant outbursts of violence can occur if social unrest were to occur. The concept of kill or be killed could apply. It would mean lots of violence, limited supplies, and lots of chaos. In the end, only those that were really prepared both physically and mentally would have a chance to hold out until some balance could be successfully restored.

Tsunami (depending on where you live)

In areas where there is an ocean or a lake, a Tsunami can occur. The large amounts of water combined with force can cause destruction of homes, food being grown, and the loss of life.

Virus Epidemic

There are plenty of viruses that have been around such as the flu, West Nile, and others that make people very ill. Only a small amount of people have actually ever died from them. However, there is the risk that there could be a virus that mutates and that it results in an epidemic of people dying due to the lack of a vaccine being available to fight it.

Water Shortage

Studies indicate that water shortages could wipe out over half of the world population. In addition to water shortage, there could be issues with water that is polluted and results in serious diseases that cause death.

These are just a handful of some of the scenarios that could play out, so you need to be ready for anything and everything. While you may not want to think about what could go wrong, you do need to think about your role and your responsibility to your family. They will be looking to you for guidance and survival.

Being able to provide them that comfort and that direction is going to give you peace of mind. The end result isn't so much what happens but how you are able to cope with it and how you are able to thrive in spite of it. The right supplies, physical abilities, and the right mindset are important to think about.

Items to have Stored

This chapter can serve as a checklist of items you need to have stored. Some of the categories also have their own chapters where more information will be expanded upon. Covering all of the essentials first is important so that you can survive the end of the world.

Food

Store food that will last for a very long time. Canned goods, dried goods, and other similar products are ideal for this. It is recommended that you rotate your stock of items periodically. This means that you consume what you have had the longest and replace it with items offering a future expiration date.

Keep in mind that you don't really know what type of natural disaster you will have. Therefore, you can't be sure you would have electricity so you need cans with pop open lids or you need a manual can opener available. You may not have heat either to warm up food so consider items that you will be able to eat right out of the can if necessary.

Keep enough food on hand to feed your family for at least 2 weeks. If you have small children, make sure you have food that they will consume. If you have an infant, formula, baby food, and other similar items that they will need to thrive are very important.

Even if that child breastfeeds, you need to have such items on hand. Remember, you are preparing for the worst-case scenario. What if the infant's mother dies or is seriously injured? What if her body stops producing milk due to the stress and the changes in diet? Be ready for anything to increase the chances of overall survival.

Don't forget food for your pets either! Many types of dry pet food can be stored for a very long time. However, canned pet food has a much longer shelf life. You absolutely want to refrain from sharing food that is stored for the family with pets so make sure you don't forget about putting away items for them too.

Water

You need to have bottled water stored for everyone for at least a period of 2 weeks. Ideally, you should have 1 gallon per day per person. This should cover their drinking needs, hygiene, and for cooking. If there is a medical concern, some of the water may be needed to clean up blood or to cleanse wounds too.

Once again, if you have pets, you will need to store

water for them as well. A gallon a day per pet should be much more than sufficient. Since you don't know what the weather will be like, it may be very hot which increases the water intake for everyone. Better to have too much than not enough.

Shelter

If there is an end of the world disaster, you will need to have shelter. You will need a place to stay warm from the elements as well as cool from other elements. It would be nice if you were going to be able to stay in your home, but that isn't assured.

Have blankets, pillows, cushions, etc. in the basement of your home where you can access them. If you can stay in your home, you may not be able to stay upstairs out in the open. You need a hiding place perhaps and the basement may be the best place in your home to have that level of security offered.

Have some pup tents ready to go as well as

backpacks. Should you need to make the decision to leave your home, you need to be able to take those items with you. The idea is to have a type of shelter you can put up just about anywhere without it being heavy or bulky for you to carry with you.

Medical Supplies

A fully stocked first aid kit is essential to have with your end of the world survival items. You don't know if someone will be injured and you need to be ready for that to happen. Some basic supplies to have available include:

- Antibiotic Ointment
- Aspirin
- Bandages
- Burn Cream
- Eye Wash Solution
- Gauze

- Ibuprofen

- Rubber Gloves

- Scissors

- Splint

- Stitching Kit

- Thermometer

Medications

If you or any member of your household takes ongoing, daily medications, have enough of them to last for 2 weeks at least. Don't wait for your medications to run low or completely out before you get them refilled. Keep all medications in the same location so that they can be grabbed should there be an emergency situation.

Keep over the counter products too including ibuprofen and vitamins handy as well. Keeping your body healthy and reducing the risk of illness or lack of energy is going to be very important. If you have children, make sure you have common medicines for them too including cough medicine and pain relievers.

Think about what you keep in your medicine cabinet now and that you may need access to. This can include antacids, anti-diarrhea medication, allergy pills, and cough medicine.

Communication

In today's society, we have become very dependent upon the internet and cell phones for our main sources of communication. With an end of the world scenario in place, those forms of common communication will likely be cut off. You need to have some other items available including a battery operated radio and walkie talkies.

Basic Hygiene

It can't be hard to focus on the issue of hygiene when you think about your life being on the line. Yet you will need to do what you can to keep urine and feces away from your bodies and from food and water supplies. Large buckets with a hole cut into them can be used as makeshift toilets. Line them with plastic trash bags that can be tied up.

Money

Don't get too comfortable out there with just your credit or debit cards. Should an actual emergency occur, you may find it is hard to buy what you need with them. Computer systems may be down so getting cash from an ATM may be out of the question too. Keep a good amount of cash in a variety of denominations with your supplies.

Miscellaneous

There are some miscellaneous items you need to have available too as part of your supplies. They will help to ensure you can take care of things and increase the odds of overall survival. They include:

- Adjustable Wrench

- Baby Wipes

- Batteries

- Binoculars

- Chisel

- Copies of important documents

- Dust Masks

- Flares

- Flashlights

- Fire Extinguishers

- Lanterns

- Matches

- Plastic bags

- Pick

- Shovel

- Whistle

- Work Gloves

Transportation Options

Initially, you may be able to stay in your home, but that isn't going to be something you can count on long term. You may need to have transportation options for small trips away from home or to completely relocate. Here are some transportation options to consider.

Keep in mind that obtaining fuel may become a huge factor. Initially, some of these transportation options may be a good idea but then when the fuel supply runs out you could be forced to use an alternative option.

Car

Using your own vehicle is going to be the most common choice. It is a vehicle you are familiar with and that you can take with ease. If you are considering upgrading your vehicle in the near future, consider one that is solar powered. This can help you get around the problems with a lack of fuel in the case of a serious catastrophe.

Pickup

If you own a pickup, that can be a better choice than a car. A pickup is going to be able to clear areas where a car may get stuck. If you need lots of room, a pickup with a full backseat area may be what you need to invest in.

The best of a pickup can also give you a place to pack up items from your home that you need to take with you. When you are in transit, you don't know the level of damages or the accessibility you will have to supplies. Therefore, it is best to take essentials with you.

Reinforced Vehicle

Depending on the situation, you may not feel completely safe in a common car or pickup. You may need to do some reinforcements with wood, metal, or steel around it. You may need to create some type of cage around it to keep others out. Hopefully, you are good with tools and you will have some access to various items.

You can also look around town for an old delivery truck. They don't have many windows in the back and they are heavy. These can give you a good framework to use in order to successfully create a reinforced vehicle. Plus, with the extra room it offers, you can convert part of it to a shelter area until you reach your destination.

Tractor

If you are in an area that has been affected by lots of rain, typical vehicles may get stuck in the mud. A tractor though can be a great choice due to the bigger tires. These machines are built for moving through the ground when it is wet or dry so it can help you avoid being stuck.

Heavy Equipment

While it will be slow moving, heavy equipment may be the answer to your transportation needs. If there has been significant damage including trees or power poles down, then you need something heavy duty. You can use such equipment to get yourself to a clear area, then look for a vehicle you can take the rest of your journey.

Semi-Truck

A semi-truck can be useful because of the power it offers, the additional room, and many of them even have a sleeper in the cab area. The downside though is that this type of vehicle does burn through quite a bit of diesel fuel. Still, it may be the mode of transportation that can at least get you moving in the right direction.

Hiking

Moving on foot may be the only real choice you have during some end of the world survival scenarios. If that is the case, grab the backpacks you have with essentials and get moving. Make sure you have good shoes for walking and clothing that allows you to add or remove layers depending on the temperatures.

Bicycle

A bicycle can be a great alternative to walking or hiking when possible. It can help you to cover more distance in less time. A bike that has several gears can also help you to get where you are headed without using as much energy.

Motorcycle

If the weather conditions are right, a motorcycle or scooter can also be a good transportation resource. This is going to use very little fuel so that is a bonus. It can also be used to move around objects such as vehicles that are stuck in the road or a tree that is down.

Horse

If you live out in the country, you may have horses in a stable or barn. You can ride them to get to your destination. Keep in mind that they can become tired though and you will need to be able to find sources of food and water for them along the route.

If you have a wagon, you can hook up horses to pull it for you. A wagon can offer more room for your family. You may not have enough horses for everyone to ride them alone. You can also use the wagon for a place to sleep and for a storage area for supplies you need to take with you.

Boat

If the waters are safe enough to access them, a boat can help you to get to where you want to go. Perhaps you know a secluded island not too far from shore where you can find shelter and be alert to anyone approaching you from all directions.

If you don't have your own boat but you can get to a dock area, there may be plenty of them you can access. During a time of natural disaster or the world coming to an end, it is every person for themselves. This means taking what you need in order to survive if you don't own it or have legal access to it prior to that point in time.

Plane

Access to a small plane can help you to get away from harm and to another destination in very little time. However, very few people have the luxury of such transportation at their fingertips. Issues such as fuel and even monitoring in air space locations though can be reasons not to do so.

Communication Options

Being able to successfully communicate during such an event is very important. It can be crucial in your efforts to decide if you should stay put or you should venture out. Communication can also give you information about what actually happened and that can determine what supplies you are going to need for the long term.

For example, if it is a chemical concern, then you need to worry more about water that will be drinkable than anything else. If the issue has to do with government rationing then you will need to do your best to conserve food, water, and to hide your weapons so that they aren't confiscated.

Radio

A radio is going to be a very valuable asset during an end of the world fall out. It can allow you to hear what is going on and to know if it is safe to come out of your home or not. If there are rescue efforts in place or a central meeting location, you can get that information too and then make a plan to be seen or to get to that location for help.

It is recommended that you have a radio that operates on batteries. You should also have a second radio though that is a hand crank model. These allow you to generate energy by cranking the handle. Don't rely on just one radio because if you run out of battery power or there is some type of failure with the radio, you don't want to feel like you have been cut off from the rest of the world.

The unknown can make your mind uneasy and stress

you out. While you may not like what you hear on the radio, it gives you something concrete to wrap your thoughts around. You don't want to make assumptions, and if you don't have a radio you can be in a position where you have to make blind decisions.

Walkie Talkies

Being able to communicate with your family or with allies is going to be important too. The use of walkie talkies is the best way to do this, but they don't have the best radius for a signal. You have to be within a small proximity for them to work. However, they can be a valuable tool for scouting, for surveying, and even for keeping watch.

It is also recommended that you have two types of walkie talkies available. This includes those that operate on batteries and then those that are a hand crank style. Once again, you don't want to rely on only one and then find out it isn't going to work. You should get walkie talkies that have several frequencies too so that you can change the channel if you have too much interference.

Morse Code

The only way that Morse code is going to work is if you are familiar with it and so is the party you send messages to. If you were in the military though or you learned this form of early communication, it can come in very helpful for you. It isn't too late to learn Morse Code either. In fact, it can be fun to test your skills with it.

Signs & Banners

Putting signs outside of your home or a building to show where you are can help search and rescue find you. It can prevent you from being overlooked in hard to identify areas. Hanging a banner outside can be a very good idea.

Signs can also be used for communication by holding them up. The other party may need to have binoculars though on the other end to be able to read them. Hopefully, you have a pair in your supply kit. Paint can be used to create messages too if you don't have a way to write on boards or other materials that will be visible enough.

Flares

The use of flares can send a message that you want to be found and that you need help. It can be very useful in the dark or when you aren't able to successfully use any of the other methods of communication in order to reach out to others.

Energy Options

What did you do the last time that the power went out? Many were scrambling for options to get some light, to make dinner, and to have some heat or air conditioning. In some instances, that lasted for a few hours or a couple of days. Now think about it on a much wider scale.

How are you going to be prepared for creating energy during an end of the world issue? There isn't going to be power back on the grid any time soon so you will have to have some great options in place that allow you to make a difference and to get what you need. Here are some energy options for you to consider:

Generator

A backup generator isn't cheap, but it can be the ultimate resource that you are glad you have should you need to create power for a long period of time. There are several sizes, so you need to do your homework before you purchase one. The amount of power that is created depends on the size of the motor that it offers.

If you have an older generator, it is a good idea to have it serviced annually. Make sure it is in good working condition. You don't want to assume you will have this to use as a resource during a disaster and then it doesn't work for you and you are stuck without a way to create a large amount of energy.

Solar Energy

So many devices today allow for solar energy to be used. This involves a collector cell that is outdoors during the sunlight and then it can be converted into energy. You can find solar powered lanterns and flashlights. During the day, they can be placed outdoors to collect the sunlight. Then at night you will have the energy collected to offer even light until the sun comes up again the following morning.

Solar energy can also be used to recharge some types of batteries. The batteries get placed into a recharge dock station. The dock station is solar powered and that is what provides the juice for the batteries to be successfully charged up. Always have enough batteries on hand that you can use some and have some in the recharge station.

Many types of cell phone charger and hand held

radios also rely on solar energy. It isn't known if your cell phone provider would still be providing any service, but in the event they can, you need to have a way to get that charge through a simple source of energy.

Chopping Wood

You may be able to chop wood in order to create energy that you need. Make sure you have tools to get this done including a sharp axe and then some smaller axes that allow you to cut the bigger pieces down. You will need to make sure you have a safe place to build a fire though. A fire that gets out of control can create more problems for your chances of survival.

Ice and Snow

To offer some refrigeration, you can rely on the elements during the colder temperatures. This includes ice and snow in order to keep items cool.

During the summer months, you may have to dig holes or find an underground basement area where you can keep items cooler. It can be tricky to do so but there are plenty of alternatives. It really depends on the climate where you live too regarding what you can count on throughout the year for survival.

Windmills

Another type of alternative energy is the use of windmills. If you live out in the country, you can put them in place. The amount of energy that is created depends on the volume of the wind. Even if the windmills are turning slowly, they still create some energy that can be used.

Weapons to Consider

In order to survive, you may need to have weapons available that you know how to use. They can help you to survive an attack by animals or by other humans. They can also help you with hunting for food or with protecting your supplies from those that didn't prepare and now they are desperate to take what they can from others.

Here are some types of weapons that you should consider. Make sure you know how they work and that you have plenty of options. Don't rely on just one type of weapon. Should it get confiscated, not work properly, or it proves to be inefficient for the type of disaster, you need a good back up plan.

Guns

There are quite a few types of guns that you can consider to have on hand. You may have shotguns or rifles around that you use for hunting or for sporting clay events. Perhaps you have a small pistol that you use for personal protection. Any of these types of guns can help you to be safer.

However, not all guns are designed well for hunting when you need food. For example, a shotgun that may use bullets for sporting clays would destroy most small animals that you could be hunting. You would need to have guns that take small ammo so that you could hunt with them successfully.

Ammunition

Of course guns are only going to be a powerful resource in your weaponry line up if you have enough ammunition for them. Many people are struggling right now to find 22 shells and other types of ammunition. As a result, you may want to pick up what you can, when you can to have enough on hand.

Another option is to reload your own. You can buy the primers, powder, and wads to use. There is a reloading machine that you will need to purchase and you will use the hulls from shells you already used previously. Remember, you aren't going to be able to just walk into a store and buy more when you run out of bullets so reloading can offer you a sound option.

Reloading isn't difficult, and you can find step by step instructions both online and in books. It does take some practice but you will find it is a great way to save money and to have the ammunition you need both now and should there ever be a need for you to use them in order to survive an end of the world scenario.

Bow & Arrow

With a bow and arrow, you can hunt for food. You can also do bodily harm to animals or humans that could be a threat to you. With a bow and arrow, you will need to have a scope and a few other accessories to ensure your aim is on target. You also want plenty of arrows because you may not be able to find those that you overshoot or that end up in the body of another living creature.

There are plenty of styles and sizes of bow and arrows out there. Many of them have adjustable arm lengths and tensions. This means that more than one member of your family would be able to use it successfully. Get one now and practice with it. There are plenty of ranges and targets out there that will help you to hone your skills with such a weapon.

Knives

There are so many types of knives including the design and sizes of them. These can be great weapons as they can fit into your pocket or around your belt. If you need the element of surprise on someone, they may think you aren't armed so that knife can be very handy.

Knives can also help with cutting ropes, carving, and creating sharp sticks or shanks that you can use for additional weapons. Knives can be used for skinning animals that you kill and cutting up meat so that you are able to prepare meals. In the event you lose your can opener or it no longer works, you can use a knife to open up canned goods as well as other packaged supplies.

Explosives

Creating your own explosives can be dangerous if you don't know what you are doing. This should only be done after carefully exploring options and making sure you have the right products on hand. Explosives can help you to clear an area, to get away from danger, and many other types of scenarios.

They can even be used to open up doors to get into a store or other locked vicinity should you need additional supplies and all laws have gone out the window due to the situation that has unfolded. Make sure you create the explosives in such a way that they won't go off until you want them to. For example, those that have a timer or that you pull a pin in order for them to become activated.

Chemicals

Various types of chemicals can also be used as weapons, but you need to make sure you don't get them on your skin. You also want to avoid breathing them in. It can be dangerous to work with chemicals if you don't know what they are able to do. You also never want to mix any types of chemicals together as that can create a very dangerous reaction.

When you know how to use chemicals correctly though they can serve as a significant weapon for you that others don't have the right knowledge about. There is plenty of information out there that you can read about that will help you to prepare for storing and using these types of chemicals as weapons.

Snares and Traps

With the use of snares and traps, you will be able to get food. You will also be able to keep people away. Without electricity, you can't rely on a home security system. You can't stay up all night either but you can put traps out there that will catch someone if they try to get close to your shelter.

Shelter on the Go

Previously, we touched upon the fact that you may not be able to stay in your home. You may need to leave it behind in order to be safe. Shelter on the go is going to be important. It will provide you some safety from the elements and from wild animals. There are quite a few options you have to consider. They include:

Pup Tents

When you travel by foot, you need to keep it as light as you can. Pup tents set up in a matter of minutes and they don't take up much room in your backpack. You can put them up when you stop for resting. They are easy to take down so you can keep moving the next day again.

If you have a vehicle, you can use larger sized tents.

You may even have items such as cots and sleeping bags with you. It all comes down to how much room you have and the essentials you are able to take along with you.

Large Sized Vehicles

If you have a large sized vehicle, you can convert part of it into a place for shelter. You can put a makeshift bed and other materials in there. This means you can drive until you are tired and then you can rest without having to worry about finding a place to sleep for the night.

Emergency Shelter Centers

With your radios, you should be able to hear information about where emergency shelter centers are set up. Getting to one of those destinations such as a football field or other large area may be simple or it may prove to be difficult. It all depends on where you are and what type of disaster has occurred.

In some scenarios, you want to remain on your own and not go to an emergency shelter where they would keep tabs on you. If you have your own supplies then you would be able to survive on your own and not be subjected to such control and outcome.

Lean To

If you don't have a tent, you may find yourself in the wilderness with just a few essentials you can use for shelter. A lean to can be created out of trees, sticks, and other debris. It offer shelter that has only three sides with a large entrance. Make sure you build it in a direction that keeps you safe from the elements.

Cave

If you happen to come upon a cave or dwelling, you may be able to use it as shelter. You do want to make sure it isn't home to some type of wild creature though that is going to become aggressive if you are in their territory.

Ditch

One of the really simple places for shelter as you are walking is in a ditch. Just make sure it isn't one that would have water running through it. A ditch offers you a lower place from the leveling of the land. This can protect you from the wind and other elements.

Being in a ditch can also help you to remain well hidden from other people who may be traveling. You aren't going to know who you can trust so you don't want to be caught off guard as you try to get some sleep.

Wagon

A wagon can offer you shelter, and if you are relying on horses for transportation it is a great combination. If you don't have a cover for it, consider making one out of tarps or other materials. This will help protect from the elements including the wind and the cold when you are sleeping.

Rest Areas

There are plenty of rest areas all over the place, even in small towns and they can offer shelter. They can offer an indoor location that you could use for shelter. This may not be the most comfortable though due to them featuring concrete flooring.

Fallout Shelter

There are still fallout shelters that were built in the 80s due to the threat of nuclear war. They can be a great choice for shelter to get away from chemicals in the air, when the circumstances are unknown, or when there is an epidemic virus going around. If your home doesn't have a fallout shelter, perhaps you know people that do have one. We will talk in a future chapter about creating your alliances.

School

A school may be a location where you can find some shelter close to you. This can also be a place where you are able to replenish some of your supplies. Schools are large and you can find plenty of places to rest. This includes a classroom where you can lock the door and make it secure for you and your family.

The gym is an option too, but very large and very open. In a smaller area you may feel more in control and not be worried about others showing up. The school cafeteria may have some very large sized cans of food that can feed people too. Rely on those supplies before you use any of your own personal supply.

Hospital

A local hospital can also be a wonderful place for shelter. There are beds, couches, and waiting areas where you can relax. If you are in need of medical supplies then you can replenish them while you are there too. A hospital is going to have vending machines and a cafeteria where you can find food supplies you may need

Clean Air

We take many things that our bodies engage in for granted. Perhaps the most common one that falls into that category is breathing. Yet it can become a key to survival if there is a catastrophic event that unfolds. Being able to get access to clean air may make the difference between life and death.

Fallout Shelter

A fallout shelter can come in very handy in this type of scenario too. You can stay inside and not be exposed to the negative elements that may be in the air. Poisonous gases that can destroy the central nervous system are important to avoid. They can result in a slow and painful death.

Gas Masks

You may want to consider having a gas mask in place for each of your family members. This can allow them to breathe in air that is safe but not harmful for them. In the early timeframe after a serious event has occurred, it is important to take all precautions. If you aren't sure if the air is safe or not, a gas mask is certainly warranted.

Facial Masks

Another type of mask you can have available are those that people wear while painting. This is known as a respirator, and there are also those paper masks that medical professionals use. All of them help to prevent harmful elements from being part of the air you breathe. There can be lots of dust settling for days or weeks after a natural disaster.

For example, think about the World Trade Center attacks. The amount of ash that was falling all around was very dangerous for people to be inhaling. Some survivors continue to have lung problems today as a result of it. The use of such facial masks can help to keep you and your family breathing in air that is debris free.

Secure an Area

It is a good idea to secure an area of your home or your shelter that you will use. If you are in a large home or a large building, use plastic and duct tape to seal of areas you don't need. This will significantly reduce the risk of contamination coming in. Seal off any cracks or drafty areas too so that they don't allow contaminated air to seep in.

Secure Windows and Doors

Don't open windows or doors unless you absolutely have to. Secure them so that they remain closed and that keeps out the harmful elements. Even if you only open these entry points for a brief period of time, you increase the risk of serious health problems for all individuals that are inside.

Air Conditioners and Fans

If you still have a source energy at your shelter location, run air conditioners and fans. They can help to keep the air circulating in the shelter. They can also reduce the risk of someone getting ill from dust and other elements that may be present.

Vacuum

Even with the location sealed as much as possible, dust particles can get inside. Vacuum twice a day if you have an energy source at your shelter location. Avoid using a feather duster or a broom though as that can stir up more dust into the air and create breathing difficulties.

Not Feeling Well

On a side note, you may experience feeling dizzy, lightheaded, or like you need to vomit. These can all be signs that you aren't getting enough fresh air. There can be gases in your home or other shelter locations that you can't see or smell but they adversely affect your body. Immediately move to an open area where there is plenty of fresh air circulating.

Potassium Iodide Tablets

It is a good idea to have Potassium Iodide tablets available. They can be taken by all family members for a couple of weeks if you feel that you may have been exposed to radiation, various types of gases, or chemicals. These pills can prevent the symptoms of exposure from becoming severe as they will protect the functionality of the thyroid.

Understanding Isolation and Quarantine

It may be necessary to separate people in your group if health issues develop. This can be emotionally very difficult. However, it may be required at some point for survival of those that are well.

Isolation is done to help stop the spreading of the problem. Some of the symptoms of lung and air related issues include:

- Chronic dry cough

- Chronic thirst

- Coughing up phlegm or blood

- Loss of energy

By moving them to an area where they aren't in contact with the healthy individuals can prevent it from spreading to the remaining individuals. Those that have been isolated may recover in time but the idea is to keep the healthy as healthy as possible so they can provide food, water, and other items for all.

The process of quarantine actually has to do with those that are well. These are individuals that may have been exposed to ill individuals. The quarantine period is to observe them and to see if they also become ill. It can take several days or even weeks for symptoms to appear. The idea here though is also to help with reducing the spread of health issues that can reduce the overall chances of survival.

Accessing Food and Water

After Disaster Strikes

Successfully allocating and rationing both food and water after disaster strikes is very important. The body can't go long without water, so that is the most essential item for survival. Yet not all water is going to be clean enough to drink. There are some things you can do to have water. This includes:

Store Lots of Bottled Water

Prevention is the best method to ensure you don't have a shortage of water. Make sure you have lots of it stored up. Water that is in sealed plastic containers are going to be safe until you use them. Water isn't going to spoil so this is a commodity you can store for a very long time.

If you have to leave your primary shelter, find sources of bottled water along your route. Any time you stay at a new shelter, go through the premises and look for extra sources of water you can take along with you. If you go by stores that are no longer operational, then you can take the water you need. If they are operational, use some of the cash you have to buy water before it is all off the shelves.

Boil Water

If you have to access water from streams, lakes, or other bodies of water, you can boil it. This will help to remove impurities from it. After the water has boiled for a full two minutes, remove it from the heat. Then allow it to cool to room temperature before you drink it.

Water Purification Drops or Tablets

There are drops and tablets that you can have as part of your emergency supplies that will help with purifying water too. You just add a few drops or one of the tablets to a specified amount of water.

Make sure you carefully follow the directions. You don't want to waste those precious drops or tablets. Yet you don't want to not use enough and have a false sense of security that the water is safe to drink when it actually isn't.

Chlorine Bleach

If you don't have such tablets available or you run out of them, add a small amount of chlorine bleach to the water. Use 1/8 teaspoon per gallon of water if it is clear. If the water is cloudy, add ¼ teaspoon per gallon.

Dig for Water

If you aren't able to find water on the surface, you may need to dig for it. You can use various tools, rocks, and other items in the wilderness to do so. You may have to dig for a long period of time before you find water.

Trees

In the mornings, trees may collect lots of dew. Of course it will depend on the location and the climate for that particular time of year. While the trees won't offer you too much water, they are better than nothing when you are in a pinch to prevent the body from becoming dehydrated.

Collect Rain Water

In the rainy season, you can opt to collect rain water in clean containers. This allows you to have some water that you otherwise wouldn't be able to. Even if you still have some bottled water around your shelter, you should consider this as it will prolong that supply.

Food Supplies

As previously mentioned, you need to have a very good supply of food that you can access when there is a disaster. Remember, it may be at a month or longer before you can leave your shelter so you need plenty of food. Some items to have on hand include:

- Baking Soda

- Beans

- Beef Jerky

- Canned Fruit

- Canned Meat

- Canned Vegetables

- Cooking Oil

- Dried Milk

- Dry Potatoes

- Dry Rice

- Flour

- Honey

- Pancake Mix

- Pasta

- Quick Oats

- Sugar

MRE's

You are going to have enough on your mind, so you don't need additional stress due to not being able to plan meals or being hungry. No parent wants to see their child go without food. Since there is no guarantee your food will be safe or that you will have ways to prepare it, you need back up resources.

MRE stands for Meals Ready to Eat, and they are very common in the military branches. There are plenty of different meal options and you just eat them right out of the package. Most of them taste decent and they will provide you with some variety. They can be purchased by the case and they store for a very long time so you don't have to worry about them being expired should you need them.

7 Day Responder

You can buy this kit that offers a 7 day meal assortment for adults. It offers

3 meals per day for that period of time. It also has snacks that you consume every day. The food items are great in taste and they are also packed with nutrition. When you are facing physical and emotional stress, eating right is very important. These pre-made meals can also be stored for a very long time.

Vegetable Garden

Have seeds ready that you can use to plant for growing some of your own food. You may be able to create a vegetable garden. You don't need to grow more than enough for your group to live on. Otherwise, it will be rotting as you may not have a way to store such food sources properly.

Take some time to learn about different types of vegetables that grow where you live. You may be surprised at what you can easily plant and grow in a garden. Of course you will need to have soil and you will need to have a decent water supply for the items to grow. You can use collected rain water when possible so that you don't use your own drinking water supply.

Hunting

Being able to use your weapons for hunting is very important. You can go hunting for many types of living creatures including:

- Bears
- Deer
- Doves
- Ducks
- Elk

- Pheasant

- Possums

- Rabbits

- Squirrels

You can use many different hunting methods in order to get those types of creatures. This can include guns, bow and arrows, traps, and snares. You may need to try a combination of different methods to see what works the best for you.

Setting traps and snares is simple enough and you can leave them while you go search for other sources of food. Then you can go back later and check those sources for additional items that may have been caught.

Food Disposal

If you have to dispose of food items from your home due to loss of power, you have to be careful about how you do it. Allowing the food to rot in the home can create a terrible odor. If you toss the food items into the trash, they can attract large animals and even rodents that are searching for food for their own survival.

The best way to dispose of food that may have been compromised is to dig a large hole at least a foot deep. Place the food in it and replace the dirt. Then cover the top of it with something that animals can't remove. This will prevent them from digging at the source of where you buried those food items.

If it isn't possible for you to get outside to bury the spoiled or contaminated food items, place them in an air tight storage container. This will help to reduce the risk of a smell coming from them.

General Survival Skills

You will need some general survival skills in order to help you get through such a crisis situation. Use this chapter as a checklist to help you get thinks in order. If you don't feel confident that you have the right skills for general survival, you need to make it a priority to develop them. Any weak link in your plan can result in you not making it.

Plan for Anything to Happen

There are plenty of "what ifs" to consider when it comes to the end of the world. With that in mind, you really need to be prepared for anything. In reality, it doesn't matter if it is a chemical warfare situation or an alien invasion. You need to have a plan that is solid and that you can follow through with no matter what.

That also means you have more than just a Plan A to

work with. Think about the variables along the way. For example, in a previous chapter we covered transportation. Location, circumstances, and even time of the year can all influence what you decide to go with.

Get your Supplies Ready

Don't say that someday you will get your supplies ready. Make it a top priority so that you can have peace of mind that you do have everything ready to go in order to get results if you need them. In a previous chapter you will find a list of all the essential items you should have on hand. If you have others you would like to add, that is fine, but don't leave out any of the listed essentials.

Rationing Supplies

Your overall plan should include how to ration your supplies. Since you have no idea how long you will need to depend in them, you need to make sure food and water isn't being wasted. The long stretch of time without things to do can get the best of people. It can also make them reach for food or water when they really aren't hungry or thirsty.

They may be doing this out of survival mode, and they need to train their mind to be sensible about it. A schedule of what will be consumed, how much will be consumed, and how food will be prepared is important. This also prevents people from fighting over supplies.

Don't skip meals or go without water through in order to save it. You are going to need to keep your immune system as healthy as possible. You can't do that if you aren't giving your body what it needs.

Rotate and Inventory Supplies at Regular Intervals

From time to time, you need to rotate your inventory of supplies. This is very important with food and with batteries. Make sure items you have such as flashlights and radios work properly. You can consume the food items and use the batteries in your home or business. As a rule of thumb, don't remove anything from your supplies until you have a replacement for it.

Keep an inventory of your supplies so that you always know what you should have. It is also recommended to keep items in different locations. For example, don't store all of your food and water in one area of the basement. If there is a problem such as structural damage, you may not be able to access that part of your home. Those supplies would be completely off limits to you.

Communicate your Plan of Action with all Parties Involved

You can't be the only one that knows of the plan of action you have for an end of the world scenario. Those that will be with you need to know what their role will be. In a future chapter, we will cover creating alliances and the dynamics that creates for your overall survival.

However, what will you do if there is imminent danger and your kids are at school, you are at work, and your spouse is running errands? A plan of action that ensures everyone can get into contact with each other and get to the meeting spot is important. The last thing you need is the stress of not knowing if someone you love and care about is okay or not.

Trust your Gut

You are going to have to make some life altering decisions, and you can't be second guessing yourself. Trust your gut instincts and do what you must to survive. This can include taking actions you normally would never be engaged in during the normal course of your life as you know it today. Make decisions based on the information you have in front of you because time may not be a commodity you have lots of.

Basic First Aid

Access to efficient medical care can be difficult during a time of crisis. Learning basic first aid can help you to take care of your needs and those of your family during an emergency situation. A fully stocked first aid kit as previously mentioned is crucial. However, those items aren't going to be much good to you if you don't really know how to use them.

Believe you can do it

This is the time for you to fully believe in yourself 100%. Your survival depends on you taking risks, being brave, and going the distance. If you aren't confident that you can do it, you are putting yourself and those around you in a dangerous situation. Focus on the best outcome you want from any given situation, not on the worst case possibility.

People Skills

If you are going to be a leader in a crusade to survive, you have to show people you can be trusted. You have to be kind, direct, and you have to be able to delegate responsibilities. Effectively being able to communicate with others is very important if you going to get them to want to follow you. A positive attitude, showing you care, and being fair will draw people to you like a magnet.

You can't force them to follow your directions. They may resent that they have to do what you say in order to share your food, water, and shelter. This can create internal disruptions that will weaken the overall ability to survive. With that in mind, be very selective about who you work with and who you protect with an end of the world scenario.

Advanced Skills that can Help you

In addition to the basic survival skills, there are some advanced skills that can help you to thrive in a difficult environment. If you are able to take part in games, trainings, and strategies that help you to develop strong skills in these areas, then you are going to significantly increase your chances of surviving.

Hunting

If you enjoy hunting, you will find it is a key skill to surviving an end of the world scenario. You may have to hunt for food that is going to feed your family for the day. You may have to go out hunting every single day in order to make that happen. Depending on the skills you have and the types of weapons, your outcome could be very successful.

Knowing the time of day to be able to go hunting is

very important. For many animals, it happens to be very early in the morning and then again before the sun goes down. However, with others such as rabbits, the night time is the best time for hunting them. Being able to identify the types of animals that are around will also aid you with hunting.

Being able to pick up on the sounds of animals, their types of tracks, the types of habitat they live in, and even the types of droppings they leave behind can all help you with hunting in the right areas for types of food sources that are going to help your family to survive.

Scouting and Surveying

Knowing your environment will be a crucial survival skill when you are one of the few remaining out there. You don't want to be a victim, always worried about what or who is lurking around the corners. Instead, you want to take a proactive approach that allows you to have the upper hand. Going scouting allows you to see if there are others living around you.

Scouting also allows you to see if anything has been disrupted around you. Perhaps you can go the distance and put up some warning elements that you will notice if they have been disrupted in any way around your living area. Surveying around you using binoculars and other tools will also help you to stay safe.

Keep in mind that people and animals may be moving from their habitat of origin due to the end of the world scenario. They are going to do what they can in order to find food, shelter, and to increase their own chances of survival. Some of them will be friendly foe that you encounter but others could be dangerous and even willing to overtake what you have in place so you have to be on the defense until you can be confident you no longer have to worry.

Growing Food

Most of us struggle to think about what to buy at the grocery store to make for dinner day after day! We also enjoy the luxury of going out to eat now and then so we can take a break from cooking.

When you are facing an end of the world situation, you aren't going to have such options. In addition to hunting, you need to do what you can to grow your own food. You need to have skills that help you with determining what to plant, how to get the soil ready, watering, harvesting, and keeping predators out of your garden.

What you grow is vital to your well-being because you can't guarantee that your supplies will last. You can't guarantee that you will be successfully every time you go out to hunt either. By growing food too, then you have another resource to help you do your best to ensure your family does have the food they need every single day.

Martial Arts

The element of surprise may be there when someone or something attacks you. Learning martial arts in some form can give you some additional skills they won't be ready for. They may see you as an unarmed man they can overpower but your skills will show them otherwise

They may think you are a small woman and you can't

possibly protect yourself. Yet martial arts is more to do with pressure points, flexible movements, and the ability to protect yourself even in the most complex of holds that the other party may have on you.

By learning martial arts, you will be prepared more than the average individual when it comes to personal protection. These skills could mean the difference between life and death for you. It could mean the difference between someone taking all of your supplies or leaving you alone.

You can sign up for martial arts classes locally. There are classes offered for all age groups and all skill levels. As your skills improve, you may be interested in taking more advanced classes. Not only will such skills help you to prepare for anything in the future, but they are great for overall fitness and your increased sense of personal protection.

Good Cardio

Your heart should be as healthy as possible. You are going to have many challenges in order to survive something of this magnitude. Engage in activities that help to strengthen your heart. This includes running, jogging, and aerobics. This will help you to have a healthier body and to live a longer life.

Military Training

If you have been in any branch of the military, or if you currently are, you definitely have an upper hand when it comes to additional survival skills. Part of military training is being able to survive in the most unusual of circumstances. You will be able to keep your wits about you and to think both logically and creatively in order to survive.

Even if you haven't been in the military, you may wish to join the reserves. This can be a wonderful way for you to serve your country and to make some additional money. You will get free training and you usually only participate one weekend per month. This training can help you to get ready for the improbable and the impossible.

Outdoor Survival

There are survivalists who have done their homework and they are up to the challenge of living in the wild for days, weeks, months, and even years at a stretch without any problems. Taking part in outdoor survival camps, challenges, and programs can help you to develop these additional skills that you may not have thought about before.

If you feel like your lifestyle depends too much on technology such as using a smartphone and a computer all the time, you need to think about how you would survive without them. Do you have a way to determine your basic directions by following the sun? It can serve as a compass so that you don't walk around in circles or get lost when you leave your camp to go hunt for food.

Weapon Use

Stockpiling weapons to use in the event of an end of the world scenario is only part of the benefit. You need to know how to load a gun, to aim it, and to fire it. If the weapon has a scope, you need to know how to use it to get your target. You want to cherish your ammo so you need to get your target on the first shot as often as possible.

If you run out of ammo or your guns are confiscated, you need to have other weapons to rely on. Make sure you know how to use a bow and arrow so that the arrow will fly to the intended target and you don't damage the bow. You need to know how to use a knife successfully so that you are able to protect yourself.

Learning about the vital body parts on humans and on animals is also important for you to get the most out of weapons. When it comes to ultimate survival, you aren't going to be interested in merely injuring a person or an animal. When you aim a weapon their direction, you should be planning to kill them with it before they have the chance to kill you.

Being Physically Prepared

You aren't going to fare well out there trying to survive if you aren't physically prepared for it. Only in the movies do the characters look amazing after days of walking or spending the last few hours running from the enemy! In reality, you are going to be tired, thirsty, and completely out of energy due to the exhaustion of all of it.

You should always strive for your body to be in good physical condition. Not only in preparation for the end of the world, but so that you have the highest overall quality of life possible.

Schedule a checkup with your doctor if you aren't at your best and make a plan of action to make improvements! It will help you to thrive and should you need to focus on survival, you will be happy your body is going to contribute all you need.

Break Dangerous Habits

If you take part in smoking, drinking alcohol frequently, or using illegal drugs, you need to do all you can to break those dangerous habits. They aren't good for your physical or mental well-being. They can zap you of energy, reduce your cardio function, and increase the risk of serious health problems including cancer and liver damage.

Eat Well Balanced Meals

Your body gets vitamins, nutrients, and creates energy from what you eat. When you consume well balanced meals, your body won't be storing up fat. You will have energy without feeling sluggish.

Don't skip meals and make sure they aren't full of processed items or high in sugar. A low fat diet with whole grains and good carbs is encouraged. Pay attention to your portions of food too. Only consume junk food in moderation.

Daily Exercise

No matter how busy you may be, engage in 30 minutes or more of daily exercise. This helps to keep your bones and muscles strong. It also helps your body to have endurance. When you are talking about survival, you need to know your body will be able to handle the challenges. Find sources of exercise you enjoy too so that you won't make excuses not do take part in it.

Healthy Weight

The combination of eating well and daily exercise shouldn't be a short term effect for weight loss. Instead, they should be overall lifestyle habits that help you to get to and maintain a healthy weight.

Being overweight is going to hinder your ability to move quickly, to feel full with reasonable food portions, and it is going to reduce overall body circulation of blood and oxygen.

Core Training

Challenge yourself to get a stronger core for your body. This can be accomplished through various types of workout plans. Yoga is one of the most common because it is low impact. It is a great way to get the core of the body strong and that means overall your body will be better equipped for physical activities.

Weight Training

Many people assume that by using weights they will bulk up but that isn't the case. Instead, weight training is going to help you burn fat and to replace it with lean muscle mass. This is going to help you become stronger.

It is going to take a great deal of weight training at heavy weights for you to bulk up so that is only going to happen if you have a strict plan and strategy in place created for such a goal.

Manage Health Concerns

Don't allow your health problems to get out of control. Prevention is the best way to life a great life. For example, take efforts to reduce the risk of cardiovascular disease and high blood pressure. If you have a family history of diabetes or cancer, work with your doctor to do all you can to prevent such developments. Regular checkups are essential, don't wait until you don't feel well to see a doctor.

If you do have a type of health problem, do what you can to manage it. Otherwise, it can continue to spiral out of control. For example, when a person is diagnosed with diabetes it can be controlled and they can have a great life in spite of it.

However, if they don't follow the orders of the doctor, it can get worse and create a downward spiral of additional health problems for the individual.

Mentally Prepared for Survival

Your mind has to be prepared just like your body in order for you to do well out there in such a scenario. You can't thrive if you can't focus on what has taken place. You can't dwell in the past about what you had, what you lost, or even what you forgot to get ready if you weren't fully prepared for such a scenario to play out.

Your mind has to be strong and it has to be focused. Being alert in spite of your body feeling fatigue and pushed to its limits is important. Being able to focus on the future and new goals gives you something to reach for even when you feel like it may be impossible to keep going forward.

Stress

Reducing stress is a big part of getting the mind ready. You can't allow stress or anxiety to get the best of you. Of course this is easier said than done when you are seeing mass destruction all around you. Being able to desensitize yourself to what has occurred though needs to take place so that your focus can be on getting through it.

Right and Wrong

The morals, ethics, and even religious beliefs that you used to hold in terms of right and wrong have to be put aside. This doesn't mean you become cold and bitter or robotic. It just means that instead of certain things being black and white there are now many shades of gray.

For example, you would never think of robbing a

store or stealing items from a pharmacy today right? However, if there was a major crisis, would you be willing to take water and other supplies from a store for you and your family to survive on?

Would you be able to break into a safe environment so that everyone had shelter? Could you break into a pharmacy in order to get the medication your daughter needed to take daily before her supply ran out?

Most of us would be able to mentally prepare for doing those types of things in order to do what it took to get through a difficult crisis type of situation. It is very different in terms of right and wrong when it comes down to being able to survive or not.

Leadership

Taking on a leadership role can be tough and it does put additional weight on your shoulders. Yet being able to make decisions that your family will follow is crucial. They are looking up to you to help them get through all of this. If they see you are worried, scared, or confused, it is only going to create more stress for them.

Showing strong leadership skills by giving direct orders, making quick decisions, and having several backup plans in the event that you run into any problems with the initial plan of action that you had in place.

Positive Mindset

When you have a positive mindset, you will be looking for solutions at every turn. You won't let what is a challenge stop you from moving forward with your survival plans. That is often what makes the difference between those that give it their all and those that give up.

A positive mindset also is intriguing to others that are suffering to see the positive elements. They will need your leadership and guidance more than they have before as they are weak in how they see things. You can offer a shining example to them that will help to modify their own thought process and behaviors with time.

Creativity

Thinking outside of the box is going to be a great skill for the mind to take part in. Getting creative is what you need to do as a common solution may not work for a given scenario. You need to do all you can to twist and turn the gears in your mind to get results.

Being creative though isn't always easy when you are in unknown territory with so many variables to think about. You may have a limited amount of time to come up with a viable solution too.

Compassion

There will be times when you need to show compassion towards others who are struggling with survival. They may need someone to help them be strong, someone to help them get their mind straight, or even someone to help direct them to take part in something positive so that they stop looking at all of the negative.

Even in the most difficult of times, being able to show compassion is a mindset you want to have. This doesn't mean you trust everyone that you come into contact with. However, it does mean you give people an opportunity as most will be trying to survive as well, not take advantage of your position.

Basic Needs

You will find that your mental well-being is easier to accomplish when your basic needs are met. These include:

- Food

- Water

- Shelter

Being completely prepared with enough supplies and a place to go will ensure that foundation is in place. With those needs met, you will find that it is easier for you to focus on other things going on at that point in time.

Survivors Guilt

The mind can also result in you having survivor's guilt from time to time. This is the feelings of regret and sadness that you were able to survive to that point but others you know didn't. Guilt can also take over if you feel that you should have done more to help someone.

While such feelings are normal, they can be difficult to control on your own. In today's society, seeking help from a professional counselor would be recommended. Yet in a survival type of circumstance that wouldn't be readily available. You will have to be mentally strong to continue on through it in spite of such feelings.

No one said it would be easy, and you may discover that the mental side of survival is harder for you to accomplish than the physical side of it. That doesn't make you weak minded at all, it just means you care and that you are used to rules and processes a certain way and engaging in particular behaviors.

The truth is that none of us really know how we would react in a given situation until it is right in front of us. We can role play about it all day long but that a far cry from being able to initiate it in a real life or death situation

Medical Supplies and Medical Care

A first aid kit that is fully stocked is very important. In an earlier chapter we covered the items you should have in that first aid kit. You should also have a smaller kit you can take with you when you are hunting or scouting that fits into a backpack. You never know when you may experience a bite, cut, or other problem that needs some type of attention.

Medical care can be hard to come by when you have an emergency due to the end of the world scenarios. Many people panic about what they would do in such an event. They want to have the care they need in order to help them live and to reduce pain. A first aid manual is a very important item to have. It should offer step by step instructions and photos.

Here are some things you can do for basic medical

care during a time of crisis:

Childbirth

The thought of giving birth without a doctor around is scary stuff. Yet the truth is that the female body is designed to complete the process naturally and instinctively. Find a location that offers shelter from the elements and that is safe. Try to have clean clothes and a towel to wrap the infant in. Do all you can to make the mother comfortable until the baby arrives.

Use water to clean the baby and make sure it is able to cry which is a sign the lungs are clear. Wrap the baby in a warm towel so that the body temperature doesn't get too low. Do all you can to assist the mother to ensure the blooding stops and that she has a warm and comfortable place to rest. She should be up and feeling better in a few days.

She will need plenty of food and water so that her

body is able to produce milk for the infant. She should get help with the newborn as much as possible so that she is able to rest and to recuperate as quickly as possible. She may be very scared to give birth this way so someone she trusts around that can talk to her and hold her hand through it can make a huge difference.

Stitches

If a cut or a puncture is ¼ of an inch deep or more, then stitches are a good idea for closing the cut. You are going to need to apply pressure with a clean cloth first to stop the bleeding. Next you want to apply a disinfectant to reduce the risk of any type of infection occurring. Super glue can be used in a pinch if you don't have supplies for stiches.

There are personalized stitching kits you can get for your first aid supply kit. The stitches need to be made close to each other so that they hold the skin closed and they need to be tight. There will be some tugging against the skin with them but it won't be severe pain. Stitches need to be done soon after the cut or puncture or they won't be any good.

Broken Bones

A broken bone is a very serious type of injury and it can't be ignored. Efforts should be made to set the bone so that it can heal properly. A compound fracture involves the bone sticking out through the skin. A closed fracture is one where the bone is broken but not through the skin.

When a closed fracture occurs, it can be very painful and there can be swelling around that area. Applying ice to any type of break can help to reduce the pain and the person should also be given ibuprofen to help with reducing the swelling. With a compound fracture, you will have to do your best to move the bone back into position. This can be painful for the person so try to do it quickly.

Use supplies you can find to offer a type of splint so that the broken bone isn't able to move. This can include sturdy branches, rope, duct tape, clothes, and any other items you can come up with. To offer more support, the area can also be adhered to the core of the body. For example, a broken leg can have a splint that goes up the leg and around the waist.

High Fever

If you have over the counter products such as ibuprofen, you can use them to reduce a high fever. If you are in the wilderness, boil some tree bark in water and make a tea out of it. This is a natural remedy to help reduce fever that works quickly.

Bites and Stings

There are plenty of pests out there that can result in bites or stings, especially if you are in the wilderness. Do your best to wash them with soap and water. When necessary, apply some antibiotic ointment to the affected area. Examine the area to see if anything needs to be removed such as the stinger of a bee or wasp or if there is a tick.

Burns

The area around a burn is going to swell so you want to remove clothing from it. As the skin cools, clothing can stick to it so remove the materials quickly, even if you have to tear them off. Apply cool water or a cool cloth to the burn area.

Pat the area dry after about 10 minutes and apply antiseptic cream and cover it with gauze. Change the dressing daily and watch for signs of infection. Don't touch the burn area directly or pop blisters that may form.

Breathing/Choking

It is a good idea to make sure you and your family are trained in CPR. This can come in very handy is someone with you isn't breathing due to a health issue or injury. If they are choking, the Heimlich Maneuver may be necessary to dislodge the food item and open up the airways again

Personal Hygiene

Bathroom Scenario

When reality sets in for the end of the world, simple things we tend to take for granted will be gone. There won't be running water and that means even going to the bathroom is going to change. It will be the least of your worries though so you need to have some things in place to prepare for it.

5 gallon buckets with a hole cut in the top work very well for makeshift toilets in your home. Line the with plastic bags that can be removed daily and buried outdoors. It is unsanitary to leave urine and feces around so you want to make sure you do what you can to make this practice as sanitary as possible. If you have to leave your home, you will have to make do with what you find.

If you travel by vehicle, you can take along the 5

gallon buckets and have a set up for the bathroom any time you need it. If you are traveling by foot or have limited room, you may have to dig holes outdoors called biffies. They will need to be buried too when you are done so that they don't create health problems.

Toilet Paper Replacement Options

Nothing is more frustrating than when you sit down on a toilet and discover the toilet paper roll is empty! Well, with an end of the of the world scenario, toilet paper as we know it may no longer be around. Perhaps you will be among the lucky folks that has rolls and rolls of it stored up for such an emergency.

Once again though if you need to leave your home for shelter you will only be able to take limited supplies with you. Perhaps toilet paper will be high on your list and maybe it won't. There are some replacement options that can seem quite primitive but people used them before toilet paper came along. They include:

- Corn cobs

- Pages from books or magazines

- Newspapers

- Scraps of material

Dental Care

Taking good care of your teeth is going to be very important. You may have plenty of toothpaste, toothbrushes, and water to get the job done. You don't want your teeth to rot or to develop cavities that can be very painful. An infection in the mouth can spread to the bloodstream and make a person very ill.

If you don't have toothpaste and a toothbrush, use your finger daily to scrap away and debris found on your teeth. Use sharpened sticks that have been heated to kill germs as a type of flossing device. Use your finger to massage your gums daily too in order to stimulate them. Pay attention to any signs of inflammation or abscess of the gums.

Do your best to rinse your mouth out well after meals so that plaque is less likely to stick to your teeth. If a tooth is a serious problem, it may need to be pulled out to reduce the pain and to prevent the infection from spreading to the rest of the mouth. However, missing teeth can make it harder to chew food and it can also allow the remaining teeth to shift around into that empty space.

There are various types of plants that can be used to make a paste that will reduce gum inflammation and to reduce dental pain problems. It can be useful to have a book about such plants as part of your overall supplies. There are some harmful plants out there that you definitely want to avoid.

Keeping your Body Clean

The days of taking a shower at your leisure are going to be gone. Water that is for drinking is going to be very precious so you can't waste it trying to stay clean. When you find a river or stream, you can use it to take a bath in. Even during the colder temperatures you can use the water to clean your arms, feet, and your face. Do what you can to keep your body clean as it will reduce the risk of germs that cause illness.

Shaving

You may not have a desire to look like the wilderness gentlemen from Duck Dynasty. Yet shaving can prove to be hard when you are in an end of the world scenario. You may have a sharp knife you can or scissors you can use to at least cut the major growth. You may want to leave the rest on your face to offer protection from the elements.

Creating Alliances

Think about teams you work with at the office. It has its perks and serves a great purpose of making sure everything gets done. There is leadership, there is delegation, and there is a common goal all are striving for. The strengths of the team outweigh the weaknesses and that is why group work is often more productive than individual work.

Yet there can be rifts that occur because too many people want to lead and not enough want to follow. Some people are bitter as they feel they are doing more than their fair share of the work. There will always be those that take it too seriously and those that don't care at all. Finding the balance doesn't always happen and there can be conflicts and backstabbing.

This is all important to think about due to the issue of

creating alliances. In reality, your chances for survival are going to improve if you are part of a group. They can help you with food, water, clothing, shelter, and to come up with creative ideas to help all of you survive. It can be extremely tough to try to do it all on your own for you and your family.

If you don't have a family, you don't want to be alone. Social interaction is a big part of what makes us unique and what allows humans to thrive. The scene from I am Legend with Will Smith comes to mind. He was so desperate to find other humans to interact with that he was in tears talking to a mannequin in a store.

By creating alliances, you won't be alone and that can be important for your physical and mental well-being. If you become ill or you break a bone, can you care for your own needs? It would be easier for someone else to be able to do it for you.

If you start to lose yourself in terms of mental connections to all of it, can you bring yourself back? It is easier if you have someone who is in control of themselves at that time to talk with.

With an alliance, you can benefit from the strengths of each other. Perhaps the group has some hunters that enjoy it and they are very good at it. They can be responsible for getting food for the group.

Others may be great at creating shelter and they can take on making sure that it is done. Others can care for the children, gather water for drinking, or even keep the shelter safe by monitoring the perimeter with weapons to make sure there isn't an attack.

Safety in numbers is true, and it can also help with peace of mind and offering comfort. Being able to share insight, being able to share supplies, and being able to benefit from those around you is going to be very important.

Establishing Rules

In order for such an alliance to work, there will have to be established rules. It should be a democracy where everyone has a say. The majority vote wins after every side of an issue has been heard. There should be a hierarchy though of leadership that develops. The alliance can't thrive if there is in house rivalry or if there is chaos.

Building Relationships

Take your time to build such relationships with neighbors, friends, and extended family. If you can't get along with someone now on a day to day basis, there is no way that you will be able to get along with them well when it comes to an end of the world scenario.

You have to be able to fully trust and rely on everyone that will be part of that alliance. This is why it should be very controlled when it comes to who is invited to be a part of it. There should be a group effort too involving checklists for supplies, meeting locations, communication, etc. Everyone will have to do their part and no one gets a free ride in all of it.

Trust your gut when it comes to building such relationships. You don't have to justify it if you feel you can't trust someone with your life. You have ownership of what occurs for you and for your family so speak up.

When there is such an alliance formed, there needs to be regular meetings that talk about changes to the plan. Current events in the government, the economy, and even Mother Nature should all be explored. The purpose of
such meetings isn't to scare anyone but to make sure

everyone is always on alert.

Plans for food, shelter, water, transportation, and communication need to be reviewed and written in great detail. Any additions or changes to those plans should be put into writing. Everyone needs to be kept informed of such changes too so that they aren't using old plans should an event occur that results in the need for immediate action.

Risks to Think About

It can be a huge burden to find food for 25 a day instead of 4 so keep that in mind. That is a risk that is involved with any alliance like this. There may be times when things are stretched so thin but hopefully you can find enough food sources to survive.

The risk of inner conflict can occur due to differences in opinion, stress, and mental anguish. Some people just don't do well at all with such turmoil and they may become mean, make mistakes, or become aggressive when their behavior was never that way before the end of the world event occurred.

The risk of serious health problems can also be a problem within an alliance. If someone becomes very ill with a virus, it can quickly spread to others. In an earlier chapter we talked about both isolation and quarantine. Isolating those that sick from those that are well can help to prevent the spread of the disease or illness throughout the alliance.

Gaining Trust

Inevitably, there will be additional people that come along after an event unfolds looking to join your alliance. They may be in need of supplies and you have to decide as a group if you have enough that you could reasonably provide for them in terms of food, water, and shelter.

You also have to be very careful about who comes along. They could be pretending to have very good intentions but then decide that they want to overthrow what you have in place. You also have to make sure they aren't part of an organization that is going to take your supplies including your weapons as part of a round up operation.

If your alliance feels their survival is in anyway threatened by letting others in, turn them away. It can be a tough decision to make that is hard on the mind due to the guilt of what will happen to them if you don't help them. However, if you stretch your supplies too thin then you put the survival of the entire alliance on the line and that isn't fair either.

When to Break Away

You may decide down the road that being part of such an alliance is no longer working for you. Perhaps your goals and the direction you wish to take for you and your family have changed. Maybe you want to stay where you are and the alliance is moving on to a new location.

If you can protect your family, find enough food, and have shelter then you can do as you please. It isn't unusual for alliances to branch off in pieces over time. The larger the initial alliance was, the more likely that is going to be. The core of the alliance though is to get you through the initial transition period.

If you feel that there is too much tension inside of the alliance or the rules aren't being followed, that can be a good time for you to break away. It may be harder to do things on your own but in an alliance like that, the foundation is already crumbling and it is going to get worse over time so it is best not to stick around for it.

Being Alert and Ready on a Daily Basis

Being ready for anything to occur every day is important. This doesn't mean you let the risk of an unknown world out there consume your thoughts and take away your happiness. When you are alert to your surroundings, you can take action based on what you hear.

Many people never had this mindset until after 09/11/01. That day, they saw what could occur on the soil of the United States and they weren't sure if it was going to be all out war or not. They were worried they didn't know where their family was, they didn't have a plan of action, and they didn't have supplies. They have changed what they think and they are ready for all of it now.

Listen to the News

Many people have stopped listening to the news because it is so negative all the time. They don't want to hear all of the bad things that are going on around the world. Yet the news is going to be a huge resource when it comes to knowing what is taking place around you. When something major is developing, the news will report it quickly. You can't always rely on social media due to the volume of hoaxes out there.

Pay Attention to the Weather

Meteorologists are able to predict weather patterns, but they aren't always 100% accurate. If they report there is an impending storm and you need to take shelter, do so. Keep your eye on the sky too and pay attention for drastic changes in temperature as well as wind direction. They can all indicate something is about to happen.

Keep your Cell Phone Charged

Get a wall and car charger for your cell phone and keep the bars at full capacity all the time. Don't allow it to get down to one bar before you charge it. Should there be any type of emergency you may not get the chance to charge it and then you are at risk of the battery dying quickly.

Keep a List of Phone Numbers

All of the cell phone circuits may be jammed or busy and you may have to use a landline phone. Many of us don't know phone numbers for contacts as they are in our cell phone by name. Keep a written list of phone numbers that you can reference if you need them.

Have Cash in your Wallet

Always have some cash in your wallet for emergency purposes. There is no guarantee you would be able to get to an ATM or a bank for cash if you needed to in a hurry. While you should have money stashed at home, you may need to have some to spend to get there so always have at least $50 in your wallet.

Keep at Least ½ Tank of Gas

Gas for vehicles isn't cheap, and it can be a hassle to wait in line at the pumps. However, you want to always have at least ½ tank in your vehicle. Ideally, you should top it off at that point. You want to make sure you have gas to get to a safe location if you need to do so immediately.

Know Where your Family is

These days it seems that family members are all going different directions. Some may be at work while others are at school. There are after school activities, sports, exercise, and errands to run. Always know what is on the agenda for your family members. Make it a point of checking in with each other if those plans change.

Know Alternative Routes

You may take the highway or the freeway to get to and from work. However, during an emergency, those routes can be jam packed with too many cars. The roads could be blocked due to damages too. Make sure you know alternative routes that can get you where you need to go. It is a good idea to have a GPS in your vehicle so that you can type in the address of your destination from any location and get directions.

Keep Medications Filled

Don't wait until you run out of medications that you take daily. Keep them filled with enough for a couple weeks at least. Call the doctor well in advance of what you need a refill and then go pick it up. That way you will have the pills should there be any type of emergency.

Inventory

Always know what is in your inventory of items that you have stored. Write down those items, the number of them, and the location. Write down expiration dates too for items that could need to be replaced at intervals. You don't want to need those items at some point and find your batteries or your food are old and outdated so you can't use them.

Exercise

Take care of your body every single day by exercising. There are lots of excuses not to do it such as being tired, being busy, or not liking it. However, change that mindset around and focus on what you can gain from it including a better body, better cardio, and reduced stress.

Mental Strength

Strive to improve your communication and leadership skills so that you can do well in the face of an emergency event. With a high level of self-confidence, you can do what it takes to move forward rather than allowing the issue to get the best of you. Work on improving your behaviors so that you are challenging yourself to be positive, to be motivated, and to be creative.

Spiritual Self

What you belief on a spiritual level can be very different than the next period. However, you need to identify what you belief and be courageous with it. Too many people are afraid to voice it due to it being different from someone else. Embrace it so that if you were to be in a situation today where survival was at risk, you would feel comfort and peace in your choice.

Peace of Mind

Every day you should have peace of mind knowing that you have a plan of action in place that is reasonable and can be executed. You should give yourself a pat on the back for having those supplies in place and knowing what you can do to save yourself and your family in the face of a disasterous event.

Conclusion

We have all watched TV movies and seen video games that talk about end of the world possibilities. There is plenty that could happen including natural disasters, man created problems, issues from outer space that come' to Earth in a hurry, and even technology going too far. We just don't know what the future holds, so it is wise to be ready for anything.

Creating a solid plan of action with various exit points, types of transportation, shelter concepts, and skills for overall survival is very important. Thinking about the weapons you will need and the skills that can help you to use them successfully should also be part of that picture in your mind.

Without enough food and water, survival is going to be very difficult. You can't assume that there will be rescue teams out there that come along to save the day. You have to be ready to care for your own needs as well as the needs of your family. You should be thinking about the possible alliances you would like to have too.

While it may be helpful to have a number of people you can all count on, there can also be inner conflicts that develop. You have to balance the pros and the cons before you decide what would be best for you to consider. You want to do all you can to ensure your survival is very possible.

Being both physically and mentally prepared for anything is also essential. When you don't know what the risks are around you, you may feel like you are scared and alone. However, being positive, visualizing success, and counting on your mind and body to get you through all of it can really make a difference.

Methods of transportation will help you to get where you need to travel to if staying in your home isn't an option. Maybe over a period of time you will have to venture from that habitat to another in hopes of surviving due to your supplies getting low. Thinking about types of shelters and protection along the way to get to where you would like to try to survive will also play a role in your overall plans.

Communication as we know it including mobile phones and computers could be cut off with an end of the world scenario. Therefore, alternative means of communication including walkie talkies and hand held radios need to be part of your supply list.

Both your mind and your body need to be in sync to survive. Being physically fit as well as mentally up to the challenges is vital. The body can only do so much, but you need the mind to give it permission to be pushed to the limits. Otherwise, your body may be frozen in place when it should be taking action.

The mind can go into survival mode when it has to, but you have to work harder to train it to make decisions. You can't get caught up in what is right or wrong when it comes to survival. You may need to think about killing animals to live when you have never harmed a fly before. You may have to think about killing others in order to protect your family. The choices can be tough but they may be necessary to live.

Medical supplies are important to think about too. If you or someone in your family uses daily medicines, you need to always have a good supply on hand. Yet there could be a shortage for you to get them in the event of a catastrophe. Try to find out information about herbal and home remedies too in the event you can't get your hands on such medicines in the future.

Making a checklist of items you need and doing inventory regularly is important. Most of us can relate to going to the store or packing for a trip. It isn't until we are done that we realize we forgot this item or that item. While it is inconvenient, we can always go back to the store or we can buy the item we forgot to pack for our trip.

That won't be the way it plays out though with a natural disaster or any other type of end of the world outcome. You have all the time you need now to get prepared for all of it. Yet should that event occur, you don't get a chance to run out and get what you forgot. Those missing items could make the difference between survival or game over.

THE ECONOMY WILL BE THE FIRST TO GO...
SO PREPARE NOW!

Right now, most of the scenarios discussed in detail above have not yet happened. **But the one scenario that's unfolding rapidly concerns financial collapse.** The preconditions of financial armageddon are set in place. It awaits a trigger. And that trigger can come from any segment of the global economy.

If we're lucky, the damage will be contained within the economic sector of human existence. The damage will be painful and widespread but society may have a chance at recovery and renewal. It is very important to diversify your assets now before it's too late.

You will need to hold physical gold and silver coins in order to survive. Cash will still be relevant, but inflation may erode its value to such an extent that it will be worth only a fraction of its current value.

187

Physical gold and silver will rise in value as physical cash values plummet. This has been the case at the end of all major empires throughout millennia and it will likely hold true for tomorrow.

Should an end of the world scenario happen tomorrow, be ready. Most people around you aren't going to be. Don't be one of them.

If you don't have everything in motion, now is the time to make it a top priority in your life.

Don't wait until it is too late and then you will be wishing you prepared long ago. None of us has a crystal ball for the future – but you can have peace of mind if you plan for any possibility to occur.

Printed in the USA
CPSIA information can be obtained
at www.ICGtesting.com
LVHW071551210823
755851LV00021B/948